For Imra

from Abraham?

15/12/2018.

Thanks for the support.

Self-Published through Create Space.

Author: Abraham Banaddawa

Illustrations and Cover Art: Boyd Migisha

Graphic Work/Drawings: Yucel Gulmez

Acknowledgements

This little book wouldn't exist without the cooing, prodding and help of my friends.

I would like to give special thanks to Cathy, Yucel, and Nicole, whose encouragement and patience was pivotal in the crystallization of what used to just be an idea.

I would also like to say to you the reader, be ye poet, stoic, critic, or novice, thank you for picking up my book. Thank you even more for buying it.

Self Taught

Nature vs Nurture

Fish are born knowing how to swim

But birds must learn how to fly

It's natural to want love

But no one can really teach you how to love

In that respect we are all baby birds

Falling from our perches towards the ground

Desperately flapping our wings

Hoping that this time around we fly

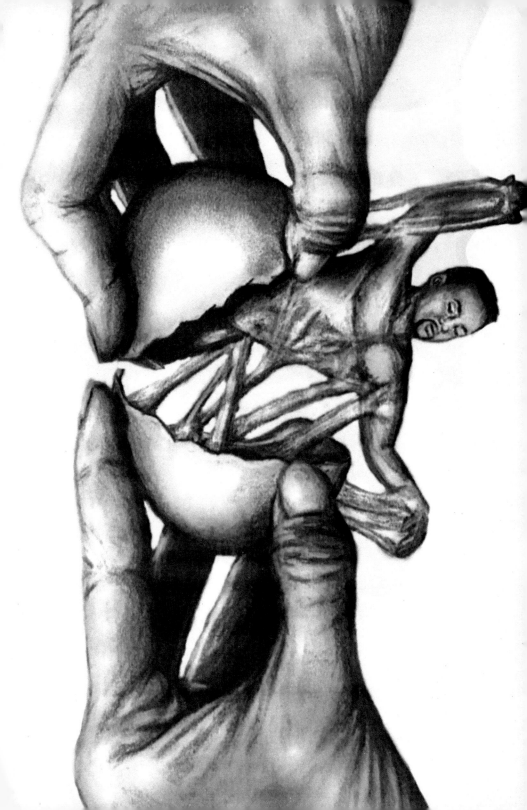

Chapters

Way back when

And...
P.O BOX #
Fledgling Love
23rd May
Words
Autumn

Not so long ago

Exile
She Killed Him Slowly
War of the Roses
10 Four

Feels like yesterday

It's OK
Fires
Far From the Usual

More recently

19 times
One Rainy Night
Solomon Grundy
Roxy
Would You Learn Chinese?
#MenAreTrash
That Type of Love

Way back when

"Autumn is a second spring when every leaf is a flower."

– Albert Camus

And...

The homie: "Dude you alright?"

Me: "I met a girl"

The homie: "And..."

Me:

"And now I am thinking that in all my freedom I was not free.

And I did not even see the shackles until she handed me the keys.

And now we are in a world waiting to be shaped by her and me.

And there need be no periodic table for us to further our chemistry.

And her anatomy has put a spell on me

And I'd happily scrap the laws of physics in favour of her physique.

And all the literature there is, exists to show that she is all that I seek.

And we speak in tongues whenever our eyes meet.

And every song seems to beat to our heartbeat.

And the histories will proclaim that there was never a love so sweet

And by the time we are through chasing our dreams the surface of the world will reassemble the soles of our feet"

...

P.O BOX

July 8, 2009 at 12:35pm

Always > at all times; ever; perpetually; throughout all time; continually without end.

It's in the air

It's stiffer than oxygen, demanding I breathe again

More than a silhouette, it's how beauty seeps from your frame,

It's the need to remember a million moments,

The smile that comes with the mention of your name,

It's the thought that popular ideals are lame.

It's the notion that not all our thoughts are the same.

It's how hours seem like minutes and minutes seem like hours,

And all those hours are ours. Just us two!

It's because with you the weather is never a topic

Who cares if it shines or showers?

In you I see the horizon as if atop a mighty tower

In you I see a garden lush with bright clover and beautiful flowers

And with you I have learned that love is power!

You have taught me to see more than I could with just my eyes:

More than the depth of seas and the tint of skies

You have shown me that all the truths of the world can't be distilled

Into lines on charts and figures in tables

And you have convinced me to listen to my heart

Whenever it says it is willing and able

As such if you'll bear

I will write to you always

Always.

Fledgling Love

Ours is a fledgling love,

Like a young rosebud in a thicket of thorns.

All I can do now is trim the insecurities

And prune the doubts that would strangle the stem.

And even as my thumbs are pricked by thorny disappointment

I shall bandage my wounds with sweet promise

And tend to my tools with passion.

I shall water the earth with truth

And as time passes and I hack away the woody insides of the thicket

That are the past fears and regrets that seek to choke your heart

I shall shine the bright light of hope and happiness through what little space there is.

And the sweat of my labour rich with devotion

Shall like the morning dew, kiss the shy rosebud

Beckoning it to bloom

23rd May

I am writing you a love letter;

A prospect that devours my ego and makes me meek.

The prospect of love true and unrelenting leaves many feeling vulnerable and weak

Instead we would rather play hide and seek

We would rather skirt the truth, flirting tongue in cheek

I am writing you a love letter;

Will you read it and see all that lies there?

See my soul quivering but defiant before the wolves of bitter rejection,

For your inspection I shall lay forth my every imperfection.

So you may see all that I have hidden from you,

So that the man that I am can be in plain view.

I am witting you a love letter;

Will you read it and know how my heart races

And sense how my eyes glow as I put ink to paper,

Know how I search for words honest and true

To convey thoughts brought on by you

Thoughts of flowers that do not wither

Thoughts of milk that does not spoil

Thoughts of rain caressing the soil

Thoughts of how my life would be complete

If in the glow of your love I did toil.

I am writing you a love letter;

Will you read it and believe that I have nothing up my sleeves

And that years after you have fallen into my arms and clambered into my bed,

I will still mean all that I have said.

Will you believe that with me, though tears may be shed you will never be misled?

I am writing you a love letter;

Will you read it and feel safe?

Safe enough to trust another,

Safe enough to go a couple of steps further than you did in your dreams,

Safe enough to sign up for all that love means,

Safe enough to cast a deaf ear to the utterances of naysayers, and their screams.

I have written you a love letter and I hope you have read it,

That it has reached you and moved you

Moved you to that bridge in the centre of the universe

Where two souls can meet and their hearts can converse

Such that through time they may traverse intertwined as two lovers

As the earth and sky do at the horizon.

I hope that you have read it, and now it's my love that you have your heart set on.

Words

February 24, 2011 at 9:39am

If there were made a word between me and you
What a word it would be;

    Said in one breath but echoing long after
    Suiting moments of grief and bringing about laughter
    Strong like amen or whimsical like happily ever after
    A word to shout out loud to the masses
    And to whisper to you softly over champagne glasses
    It would be long and pronounced with sweet syllables

    Spoken in greetings and spoken as jest
    To convey what all others do not
    Describing the yearning of my flesh
    and the beating of my chest
    Hard to pronounce but never misspelled
    With many meanings and no synonyms
    A word angels could sing,

    Its very utterance challenges how the world should spin
    So calamitous in its beauty that not to use it would be sin
    A word of healing and rebirth
    Constantly on my lips

To describe your frame, your waist, your hips

To make you smile

Inviting thoughts of romance
and having them linger a while

Distilled from pure infatuation

Glaring at the reality of our imperfections
with firm insubordination

A word to set free from my heart all that you capture

What a word it would be.

Autumn

Would you take some time to hear me out?

Take some to figure out what this fight is really about

Between the two of us we speak six languages

But you do not seem to be hearing me

I guess all those times you said we were good

I should have knocked on wood

But right now I just want to be understood

And now it's so quiet I miss the fights it's unbelievable

Is this what it feels like to fall out of love?

We used to say that was inconceivable

Why won't you just talk to me!

Stop acting like all our syllables became billable

Let me know what's going on

I just want to be understood

It's about as subtle as the leaves falling off the trees

The seasons aren't the only ones changing

I can see it in your eyes, your hearts been eclipsed

But I can't tell whether it's love that you have given up on

Or maybe you no longer believe in us

Pretty soon you will be leaving me

And all we will have in common is the desire to be understood

Not so long ago

Are feelings true?

For how could such a thing so immense and real in its moment not be true?

But then again how could a truth change?

Exile

Seems the price of my love was too steep for you to pay

Thought to shelter you in my arms but instead you sent me away

I guess the war wasn't over for my heart

For with you it chose to stay

I can understand it had more to say

It spoke your language, enjoyed your food, and danced to your songs

In short, your ribcage was the land to which my heart belonged

How could it be that now it had no home?

Cast into the cold world as a nomad you set it to roam.

Just for foreigners to come and vandalize our history

And make knickknacks and souvenirs out of proud totems

Thousands of miles away in a beautiful desert on a chilly night

My heart looks up at the night sky wondering

Do you still look up to the stars at night?

Are these the same stars you see?

She Killed Him Slowly

She killed him slowly, one day at a time.
Poison on her lips from when she stabbed him,
the dagger her kiss.

She crippled him slowly, one hug at a time.
Bludgeoned by a fading embrace,
His soul broken, bundled behind a brave face.

She burned him, one ounce at a time.
Her words sweet and painful,
Deftly scalding the bones within his skin.

She buried him, one inch at a time.
Lost in the quicksand of her wicked ways,
her actions the gruesome undertaker of his last days.

She crushed his spirit,
broke his heart and tormented his mind.
It was I she killed.

She killed me slowly
She killed me one day at a time.

War of the Roses

Slept off in a bed of roses woke up in a pile brambles,

Perhaps loving you is a bit more than I can handle,

Yet still I am addicted to this war.

To the battlefield I keep returning, like a caricature of Rambo.

When it comes to bad habits I wasn't even the type to dabble,

But here we go with you tripping me up and convincing me that I stumbled.

And day after day I am still convinced I can build cathedrals out of these shambles.

And all I really want to say is Fuck You

But that doesn't rhyme so we'll just count that as a bad example,

And when it comes to stuff you can use against me I am sure this will be heavily sampled

Just remember though,

Even the elephant starves once all the plants have been trampled.

10 Four

Have you heard of Stockholm syndrome?

Safe to say we were a little symptomatic

I sought out to catch her but, she turned it round on me.

And then she was my captor

The curves on her body like a lasso that's how she roped me

Pulled me in close kissed me and groped me

With her body she loved me with her words she beat me

But who could I tell I mean even I didn't believe me!

I was betrayed, my heart had deceived me

Pledged allegiance to she who didn't need me

It's always problematic,

Trying to explain addiction to an addict

See we were emblematic of that text book phrase

Co-dependent, that was us.

Because I hated and loved it

I gave you my all but you gave only what you could spare

I hoped you would love me the alternative seemed too harsh to bare

And still I dug deeper hoping to find treasure there

Even though deep down I knew your heart was threadbare

I put you in goal but you were never a keeper

Humour helps to mask the pain that is still present

Even though the past is where you feature

They say always be mindful of your lessons and grateful to your teachers

So cheers to heartbreak and optimism, and a toast to one heck of a bright future

Feels like yesterday

I met her,

And invited her into my room.

She hung a painting over the hole in the wall.

I call it hope,

It covers up my despair.

It's OK.

It feels like the world should be ending but it isn't, so I guess it's ok even if it's not.

So should your friends ask where we went wrong,

It's ok to put the blame on me for our tragedy.

Should you fail to sleep and the night seems longer on your own,

It's ok to call me.

Should you find the sweet caress of sleep only to see me smiling at you in your dreams,

It's ok to smile back at me.

Should we meet in the future and I seem like less of a man,

It's ok, just know that you took the best of me.

Should you be quick to replace me,

It's ok that our favourite show will still have you thinking of me.

Should you choose to forget me,

It's ok to start with the bad times and end with the good memories.

And should time pass and it no longer stings to think of me,

It's ok to forgive me.

Fires

Our love was a fire. Bright and strong, tender and warm. It drew in those who believed that there was more than the cold to be found on the hard ground. Some were inspired. And a brave few lit their own torches and set out to light their own fires. But behold one night "they" stepped in. They stomped out our fire and then they stole you away. They left me half buried and numb with nothing to feel, no warmth to speak of and with no one to hear my languishing heart.

I do not recall much of the darkness that followed, save for the things that clawed at me from the shadows. After forever and a day a pale moon drew me to the horizon where I saw a fire dim and fading. Having lost my own I could not stand by and watch another fire die. A bruised and bludgeoned emissary I stepped forward asking only to help, shouldering their embers from the harsh winds. And as they nurtured each the soft glow bloomed into a roaring blaze. As I stepped back into the night they asked to linger and to regale them with stories as they had heard of our fire that shone like a star that had fallen out of the sky.

And for a while so it went. I was an ambassador of love. I danced by fires and even lit a few of my own. For a while I was certain that the warmth of our fire would lead me back to you. But as the moons waxed and waned so did the warmth fade from my veins. It wasn't long after that, that half the memories of half the stories were all I had left.

Unprepared to accept our fate, I borrowed some embers and kindling and chased the horizon until I caught up with you. I built you a fire, and I fashioned you a stool but you would not sit beside me. You no longer cared for the memories of this romantic fool. Nor did you yearn for the soft earthen embrace of my arms or the bright warmth of my love. You no more desired to lose yourself in the deep wells of my eyes. You since became accustomed to a world that had no place for me in it. You were cold like wet coals, and as we talked sweat beaded on your brow. You could not find the strength to say it but the uneasiness in your voice told me that you would never be mine again

So I lit a torch and dived back into the woods.

Perhaps I will find another with whom to dance by the fire. Someone new to count stars with, and paint moons.

Far From the Usual

It was more like a stop sign than a red light

That's how you halted me

Like a whisper in the middle of a concert

That's how you spoke to me

Like a soft light in a dark room

That's how you looked at me

You were far from the usual

More like a fire fighter than a storm trooper

You barged in just to rescue me

I should have known it would take a fellow wounded soul to tend
to me

And with arms slung over shoulders

Like a three legged man we hobbled on

You were far from the usual

Like a great story in a foreign language

I was drawn to you even though at first I didn't understand it

And all the happenstance was so romantic

It was a beautiful type of madness

You were easy to love

And now I know never to take that for granted

You were far from the usual

Like a squatter in my heart you stayed

And like a saint you gave and gave

You were quick to forgive when I misbehaved

It was not until I became a glutton for your love

That I realised how long I had been starving

You were far from the usual

You were so strong and yet so vulnerable,

A young man who knew nothing of the world, I swore to be honourable

I was your safe harbour in trying times

And you taught me to brave the tides

And I still recall those times we missed out on star lit skies

We were too busy lost in each other's eyes

You were far from the usual

It was like that country song on the long ride home

That's how bad I wanted to hold on

But just like a rainbow at the end of a storm

The truth is us too, would soon be gone

I never knew you could be so strong

Until I saw you start to move on

You were far from the usual

And even though it's a long, long time since those days we spent

Memories of then make my heart content

And though you do not belong to me

I am grateful for your chapters in my history

And if in case you stumble across this

Know, that to me, you remain

Far from the usual.

More Recently

"At some point in life the world's beauty becomes enough. You
don't need to photograph, paint, or even remember it.
It is enough."

– Toni Morrison

I can think of quite a few times I should have kissed you

Not to mention those times I was too proud to say I miss you

There were at least 3 parties that if I tried a little harder I could have made it to.

And a couple that I left early even though you asked me to stay

I can sparsely recall,

What it was that had me so scared?

Instead of asking you to dance, I stayed quiet and still like a painting posted on the wall

Just to go home with a head full of things I could have said to you

Just to fall asleep wishing I said them all

I guess I lost sight of all those summers worrying about the fall

But there is nothing quite like the loneliness of winter to give even a shy guy the courage to risk it all

You see those moments stand tall in the landscape of my memories

Like lighthouses they dot the coastline of my mind

19 times I sold myself short and thought that you needed someone who had everything

But maybe today you could be happy with someone who wouldn't trade you for anything

Solomon Grundy

There goes Solomon Grundy

His heart still beats but he already died

His wisdom beyond his years killed off his youth

So now he hangs his head

He probably would hang himself instead if it was not so uncouth

"In a world so fake is it still noble to tell the truth,

or is truth-telling a washed up form of antiquated pride?"

He tried and he tried but his hope drowned as he fought the rising tides

He seems to have turned his back on the world

He keeps not even his shadow by his side

"If a flower bloomed in a dark room how could you trust it?"

The most efficient way to feed the world is with LED's,
but to Solomon, the thought of beautiful petals never kissed by the sun is too disgusting

"The world made man, but what is the nature of the world man is constructing?"

So Doctor, tell me what does it really mean to be alive

I too feel the cold seeping into my bones

Do not say it is nothing

If you can't explain it, at least prescribe me something!

One Rainy Night

The air got tense as I walked her to her door

She said,

"Thanks for the chivalry hero!

Now I know you're trying to be Mr. Right

But I believe in that even less than I do a god above me

Back when I was pure, the realest lie I was told

Was by a string of men who said they loved me

The truth is there are no truths in this life

Plus if you knew the whole truth

You wouldn't be trying to make me your wife

Like how I have been the other girl

While someone's wife was home, sleepless at night

This is just how this city works, don't rattle your head

And it's a long drive back to your place so why don't you just join me in bed?

You've been saying all day that I was on your mind

Well here is your chance to cross the finish line."

Like a mule I had without thinking entered her place. It was then she saw the confused look on my face and with a chuckle she said, "Stop wondering whether what we are about to do is wrong or right, either head back out the door or turn off the light"

Ticket stubs

Finding old ticket stubs in my jacket pocket always has a way of bringing back fond memories. And this morning I guess you could say I found some ticket stubs on the internet.

I am glad we went dancing on the surface of the sun.

I am glad we made the world our photo booth.

I am glad we exchanged a billion looks.

I am glad we lived like words in a book.

I am glad we made all those plans.

I am glad for all the times we failed.

I am glad we tried.

I am glad we were too boisterous to hide.

I am glad for all the new experiences we shared.

I am glad for all the habits that rubbed off.

I am glad for fights over the little things.

I am glad for our long caresses and soft kisses.

I am glad for that outrageous phone bill.

I am glad for a million inside jokes.

I am glad for the hours we spent in traffic jam.

I am glad for Gigs of social media, for links to YouTube, and for little packets sent across the room on Bluetooth.

I am glad you got to complain that I walk too slowly.

I am glad we had a long run.

I am glad you gave me reason to miss you so much.

I am glad we were so in love.

And as much as you are not mine anymore I am glad you once were, and I am certain I am better for it.

Thank you :)

Would you learn Chinese?

Would you learn Chinese?

Or Arabic? Or Latin? Or an even more ancient language?

Just to coax my soul out should my wounded heart retreat.

If I penned down my life would you dive into the volumes I placed at your feet

If I shared my fears with you would you be discrete

Would you be bold enough to answer every question that you dared to ask

Would you work things out with me or let others do the math

On the map to your heart would you get mad if I forged my own path?

Could you do more than stick around for the ride

Could you make haste so that we could waste time side by side?

Could you forgive the fact that I can't sing

And be moved that I learnt all the words to your favourite song

Would you do these and countless other things with me?

Grab a pen, here is some paper

Let's make a list a million miles long

Roxy

With all the beautiful lies, and all the terrible truths

We wind up under the upper hand

Selling our souls to a preacher man

Because we are all too scared to die

In a world that's built on denial

Where girls are told not to try

And boys are told men never cry

Where the fear of the fall,

Is louder than the call to the sky.

We wake up half dead and in search of bread

Quieting our hearts to listen to our heads

But that was never what it meant to be alive

Not for you and I

We disregard moments but cherish things

We really are strange and petty beings,

But from this pit I will sing

Bathed in the joy your name brings

And I know I will see you on the other side

When I am no longer under the upper hand

In the meantime, we can live on, you and I.

In this here lullaby

Here the memory shall be eternal,

The endless smile between you and I.

#MenAreTrash

Men are trash

Yes we have heard you and lost track of how many times you have said it

But if men are trash what of it?

Where do we head from here?

How do we raise a generation with a little less litter?

So that we can live in a world where our daughters and granddaughters have less cause to be bitter

As a man I too desire to live in a world that's better

A world where a whole gender isn't afraid and dismayed,

A world where victims instead of getting shamed get supported.

A world where the law won't let things like the length of a girl's skirt

Get rapists and child abusers acquitted.

A world where our sisters and daughters could live free.

Free of fear.

Yes men are trash, many of us do agree,

But the little boys of today should not be forgotten.

For if we raise them right we will have a new generation of men that are not rotten

We must teach them empathy and respect we must free them from entitlement and greed

We should instil that consent is a thing, and teach them to respect and honour every living being

If we make them champions of justice what a world it could be

A world where we no longer need the hashtag because the trashiness of men is history.

That Type of Love

Someone asked me, how can I be such a cynic and still believe in love?

It's because I have had a taste of real love

That so sweet your tooth aches type of love

That when your mouth's so full of syrup you slur your words type of love

That you nourish each other like honey type of love

That surprise you in the middle of the week for no reason type of love

That it doesn't matter whose party it is,

The invites stay addressed to the both of us type of love

That take you to the sports game type of love

That I don't care if you post this type of love

That I made you a mix-tape type of love

That we both so corny type of love

That "did you see the sunrise this morning?" type of love

But nowadays I would be grateful for some baking soda type of love

That wholesome but boring brown bread type of love

Because what we have is a lot of we're good for the moment type of love

And when it's over we're going to put salt in those wounds type of love

That we keeping score type of love

That we do it for the gram type of love

That you won't be here that long so don't worry about my *body count* type of love

So forgive me for not buying into that "add to shopping cart" type of love

That I don't give a damn about the environment type of love

That we don't talk a lot because you get on my last nerve type of love

That "why are we even doing this?" type of love

But I still have hope, waiting for that pacifist who knocks you out type of love

That stay up till 4 am talking type of love

That I even smile while I'm yawning type of love

That skip the toothpaste and kiss you first thing in the morning type of love

That you can eat the last of my fries type of love

That call you back right after this meeting type of love

That I hate this show but I will watch a whole season with you type of love

That join you in the gym, juice fast type of love

That there's a dent in my side the shape of you type of love

That I got to thank God for you type of love!

That will you take my last name? Type of love!

_____

_____

_____

_____

_____

_____

_____

_____

_____

_____

_____

_____

_____

_____

#ThatTypeOfLove

About the author

Abraham Banaddawa grew up in Kampala, Uganda, loves to travel, likes to cook and day dreams a little too much. He hates traffic jams, mosquitoes and people who put empty containers back in the fridge.

He is a youngish (lol) poet, an entrepreneur, and a scientist at heart. Sometimes he writes poetry to unclog, his mind, to unburden his heart, to reach across the void and touch another soul, and to respond to the challenge of a blank piece of paper. In his first book he puts together a collection of poems that tell the story of a young man trying to figure out what love is.

And at his core he is just another human being writing his story.

Find him @abrahambanadawa on Twitter.

Bonus Material

Love is...

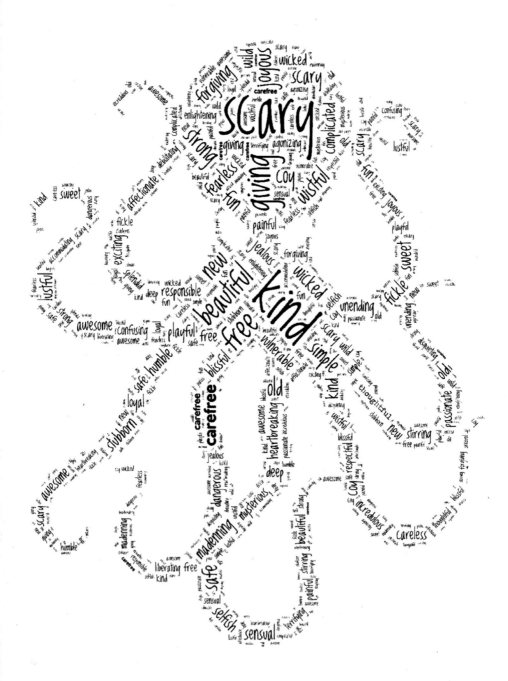